I Can Pray!

Written by Josep Codina
Illustrated by Roser Rius

PRAYING WITH LITTLE ONES

Pauline
BOOKS & MEDIA

I can pray when I look at
the wonderful world around me.

I can pray when God gives me things that make me happy.

You are my Heavenly Father, God.
You take care of me.
I love you and I trust you as I love
and trust my Mom and Dad.

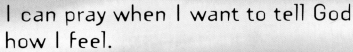

I can pray when I want to tell God how I feel.

I can pray when I've done something naughty or made someone sad.

I can pray when I need
something for myself
or for others.

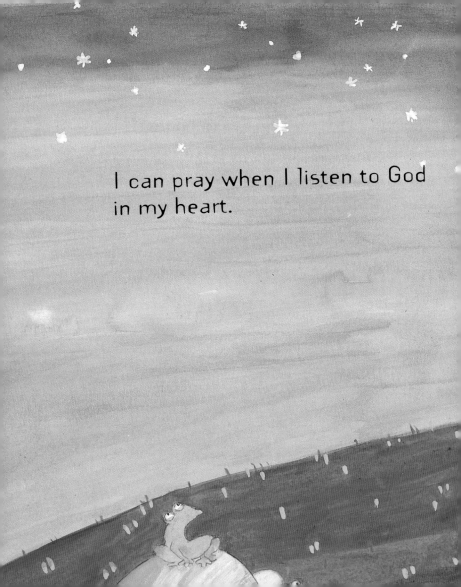

I can pray when I listen to God
in my heart.

To Parents and Teachers

You are constantly helping your child/children to learn useful lessons for life and acquire a balanced personality. A child's relationship with God is very important in helping him or her discover the meaning of life. It's also central to fostering a healthy sense of self-esteem and love for others.

Prayer is an expression of a personal love relationship with God. In order to learn to pray, it's important for your child/children to sense the presence of God in your own words, attitudes and actions. If you admire and adore God, they will learn to do the same. If you are thankful to God, your children will learn gratitude. If you show your love for the Lord by praying frequently, your children will follow your example.

The first step in teaching your child/children to pray is to encourage them to love, adore, trust, and be grateful to the Lord. This little book can help you with this, but never underestimate the power of your own lived example.

Pauline Books and Media Centers operated by the Daughters of St. Paul:

3908 Sepulveda Blvd., Culver City, CA 90230   310-397-8676

5945 Balboa Ave., San Diego, CA 92111   858-565-9181

46 Geary St., San Francisco, CA 94108   415-781-5180

145 SW 107th Ave., Miami, FL 33174   305-559-6715

1143 Bishop St., Honolulu, HI 96813   808-521-2731

For Neighbor Islands: 800-259-8463

172 N. Michigan Ave., Chicago, IL 60601   312-346-4228

4403 Veterans Blvd., Metairie, LA 70006   504-887-7631

Rt 1, 885 Providence Hwy., Dedham, MA 02026   781-326-5385

9804 Watson Rd., St. Louis, MO 63126   314-965-3512

561 US Rt. 1, Wick Plaza, Edison, NJ 08817   732-572-1200

150 E. 52nd St., New York, NY 10022   212-754-1110

2105 Ontario St., Cleveland, OH 44115   216-621-9427

9171-A Roosevelt Blvd., Philadelphia, PA 19114   215-676-9494

243 King St., Charleston, SC 29401   843-577-0175

4811 Poplar Ave., Memphis, TN 38117   901-761-2987

114 Main Plaza, San Antonio, TX 78205   210-224-8101

1025 King St., Alexandria, VA 22314   703-549-3806

3022 Dufferin St., Toronto, Ontario, Canada M6B 3T5   416-781-9131

1155 Yonge St., Toronto, Ontario, Canada M4T 1W2   416-934-3440

Original title: *Que n'ets de bo!*

English adaptation by Patricia Edward Jablonski, FSP

Copyright © 2002, Editorial Claret, S.A.
Barcelona, Spain (World Rights)

ISBN 0-8198-3682-6

Published in the U.S.A. by Pauline Books & Media,
50 Saint Pauls Avenue, Boston, MA 02130-3491.

Printed in Spain.

www.pauline.org

Pauline Books & Media is the publishing house of
the Daughters of St. Paul, an international congregation
of women religious serving the Church with the communications media.

1 2 3 4 5   06 05 04 03 02